*Unless otherwise indicated, all scripture quotations
are taken from the King James Version.*

Good Morning Your Highness
ISBN 0-970098758
Copyright 2004 by Christine Martin

Published by Dave Martin International
P.O. Box 608150
Orlando, Florida 32860

WHY I WROTE THIS BOOK:

"You'll never get ahead until you get started."

-- *Dan Scobey*

Ladies, I put this daily guide together for more than one reason... the first being myself. I have a bunch of "devotionals" sitting on my night stand, some partially marked up with ink and the rest never even opened. I wanted to write something that was light-hearted. In fact, the word devotional even freaked me out... The word sounded so intense; devote myself to daily reading and then what, would I really be changed? I am so busy, how can I possibly "devote" one minute to something that seemed to be a drag? I wanted to read something that was relatable, instead of rigid...I wanted something that I could read in a few minutes, but meditate on all day.

You can read this in the morning, at lunch with coworkers or at night. I made it small so you can slip it in your purse and refer to it when you need to. You may find that you read it out of order. If that happens, that is great! You are beginning to get it! You won't find Rules, Regulation and Religion, but you will find Reality and the Word of God.

This is my life. For so many years I have been told, "You need to be very vocal and intellectual; use power words. People will only hear you if you look and sound smarter than they are." Let me tell you, you can have all the intellect in the world, but it is your heart that matters the most.

I want to restore that childlike faith in women. Remember back when you were a little girl and you felt that nothing was wrong with your body and you had the freedom to dream? Honey, let me tell you the Prince is coming to rescue you from your Tower of Pain. He is riding on a White Horse and His name is Jesus.

My editor wanted me to "tone it down." He said, "It is too much reality; it should be more polished." Finally, in agreement we concluded real women wanted real answers to real issues.

Life is the best teacher. So grab a cup of coffee, your highness and begin your journey.

Day 1

But those who wait for the Lord
[who expect, look for, and hope in Him] shall
change and renew their strength and power;
they shall lift their wings and mount up
[close to God] as eagles [mount up to the sun];
they shall run and not be weary,
they shall walk and not faint or become tired.

Isaiah 40:31
(The Amplified Bible)

Really and truly, take this scripture and write it down on an index card and quote it throughout the entire day. It takes discipline to study the Word of God. But today, this is a simple way to help discipline you in learning to memorize and quote Scripture. You may even want to do this with all the other verses in this cute devotional book. I personally take colored index cards and have them handy in my purse or post them on my mirror were I can see God's Word before me daily. So have fun with this simple task today!

"Discipline is the bridge between goals
and accomplishment."

– Jim Rohn

Health & Beauty Tip

Going to bed at night with make-up on your face takes 10 days off the life of the face. Through the tossing and turning, the makeup gets ground into the pores and causes the grime to go deeper. The eyelashes also take a beating; they get dry and flaky and squished together as your eyes are closed for beauty rest. If you're not careful you'll look like a beauty beast in the AM. Oh gimmie a break, I'm just kidding here; just be disciplined to take off your makeup at night. Your skin will thank you for it!

"Talent without discipline is like an octopus on roller skates. There's plenty of movement, but you never know if it's going to be forward, backwards or sideways."

– H. Jackson Brown, Jr.

Day 2

*You realize, don't you, that you are the temple of God
and God Himself is present in you?*

I Corinthians 3:16
(The Message)

It took me years to realize this truth that I am connected with God. I am fearfully and wonderfully made. I had to realize that everywhere I went I took the presence of God with me. This is something to really think about…is the place you're going, a place where God would want to be?

I once had a friend who invited me to a bar. Well, this was absurd, being that I was now saved, sanctified and delivered from such a life style. They asked for my attendance and I declined! I love all people and want to help all people, but the Holy Spirit will not be in ALL places. I only remembered the way it was when I would entertain those thoughts, feelings and actions in a bar…this is no longer a part of me. That girl died a long time ago and I have no desire to raise her back up.

The Word says, "If we be in Christ, we are a new creature; behold OLD things have passed away and ALL things become new." There was a time when I would play church; enter the bars on the weekend, even talk to the people in the bars about Jesus and then love God in the Sunday services. Looking back, I realize how ignorant this truly was. My heart meant well, but my head was all wrong! When these two link up and we get a realization of who we are in Christ and how He lives in us, we would not want to do anything that would grieve Him.

However exciting that bar scene was, the closer I got to God, the stronger His convictions became in me, until I could no longer enter a bar without feeling dirty, cluttered and extremely disgusted with myself. I am supposed to be living a life worthy of what God has called me to (Ephesians 4:1 & 1 Thess. 2:12) and this was not pleasing to Him and I was the only one stopping my blessing from coming in. This does not mean that I cannot help those people who are still searching for their significance in Christ, but it does mean I have to use WISDOM and with knowledge comes responsibility.

If you happen to be one who is struggling with this very same thing, let me advise you...if you were to walk into a place where the Holy Spirit would be grieved, don't question why He feels distant or why you may feel no peace; it is because He does not dwelling in that junk. Do not pretend to be someone you are not; you are made in God's image and facing that concept is powerful. To want to be someone else is like a slap to the face of God. It is to tell God that He did not know what He was doing when He created you... EVERY-THING HE CREATED WAS GOOD! Be honest with yourself, your faults, your imperfections, everything. Celebrate the real you and love it.

"The finest clothing made is a person's own skin."

− -Mark Twain

Health & Beauty Tip

Take time out for you today. Examine yourself. Are you living life the way God would have you to? Are you too busy to even make the right decisions? Never make any decision when you are tired...take a short walk at lunch or a bubble bath when you get home...just do one thing to respect yourself today. Handle your body with care. You are the finest thing God ever created...it is ok to indulge and pamper yourself; this is only a sign of self respect. If you feel good in your skin, it shows. Just don't reveal too much skin. Ha-ha oh, gimmie a break... let's lighten up here...I have to believe that you are mature enough to understand what I am saying.

"If you follow only one rule, let it be this one: Be yourself. The really strong relationships are based on what people really are, not on what they pretend to be."

– Source Unknown

Day 3

As pressure and stress bear down on me,
I find joy in your commands.

Ps 119:143
(New Living Translation)

Before I had experienced total deliverance in every area of my life and became totally FREE, I was ignorant and not honest with myself regarding my health. I had very little understanding of the negative affects of prolonged STRESS. Meaning I would run right into it and embrace it. Stress never held me down, I just kept doing, writing, traveling, preaching...whatever life dealt me I handled it. Until I became very ill; my body caught up with me and screamed LISTEN!

I was out on the road preaching when I had to be rushed to the hospital because of a bleeding ulcer. I was bleeding internally and my body had had enough. I finally returned home and my doctor gave me some advice... "SLOW DOWN or you will kill yourself." SLOW DOWN? Was he crazy...no! He was not ignorant and neither was my body. It screamed for help long before this ulcer appeared, I just never took time to listen, instead I kept running.

After much wisdom from my doctor and a personal trainer, along with the most important helper of all Jesus...I got well and stayed well. Today, I am very health conscious and I watch my stress levels. I practice the Word of God daily; I seek Him FIRST on everything and my life has never been so complete. It almost took a tragedy to wake me up.

Thank God I finally heeded the call and LISTENED and made POSTIVE actions so I can be effective for God, my husband, family, my church and staff...every area of my life is now complete because of the Completer...Jesus. Heed His call always; don't wait until it's too late to take care of yourself. Stop running, take time out today to make God #1 in your life. He will take care of the rest.

> "A woman under stress
> is not immediately concerned
> with finding solutions to her problems,
> but rather seeks relief by expressing herself
> and being understood."

– John Gray,
American Relationship Expert, Author

Health & Beauty Tip

JUST SAY NO! (Or as Nike puts it, "Just do it!") Just be bold; don't hold back from informing your friend, spouse, in-law or whomever, that you would not like another piece of chocolate cake or in fact, you don't want one piece at all! If you are in a healthy routine, don't break it. It is ok, even if you're in a social environment, to decline any food offered to you. Remember, you manage your health, not others. It is ok, from time to time, to indulge in some ice cream or a cookie, but do not become gluttonous. Take care of your body and exercise. Do one thing tonight before going to bed, try some simple stretches or take a long brisk walk after dinner...start somewhere and document your results. (And if you have no routine, I challenge you to create one...life is only what we put into it....exercise and you'll live longer!)

"If you ask what, is the single most important key to longevity, I would have to say it is avoiding worry, stress and tension…and if you didn't ask me, I'd still have to say it."

− George Burns

Day 4

But no weapon that can hurt you has ever been forged.
Any accuser who takes you to court will be dismissed
as a liar. This is what God's servants can expect.
I'll see to it that everything works out for the best."
God's Decree.

Isaiah 54:17
(The Message)

One does not ever fail but forever learns. If you have learned what not to do from an adversity, then you have truly succeeded. I remember a time in my life, when my husband and I had hired some individuals to be a part of our team. It looked right, felt right, but was completely wrong!

Our hearts saw the good in these individuals, but our head, at that time, had a hard time discerning the truth. To make this short, it turned out to be one devastating event! Before we knew it, great discord was occurring with them and our other team members, resulting in numerous other acts (not to be discussed, but be assured, it threw us for the loop of our life!) We had a choice; we could have become angry and bitter when reflecting and analyzing all of things we did not see going into this merger OR we could see this as a great opportunity for growth.

Your enemy is only proof that Satan believes in your future; if it were not so, the enemy would not try so hard to knock you down! In the times when we over-analyze our failures, our mind keeps us from recognizing our successes. When we choose to focus on our future and use this adversity to our benefit, we gained much strength and insight and will never repeat this pattern.

Today, these individuals have been released from our team, our current staff-team members now have grown to love and respect one another in a greater way, as well as walk in unity. God has truly blessed us with our wonderful staff-team and this adversity only made the truly loyal ones grow closer. A word to the wise, never over-analyze…just learn to discern!

"Character cannot be developed in ease and quiet. Only through experience of trial and suffering can the soul be strengthened, vision cleared, ambition inspired and success achieved."

— Helen Keller,
writer, lecturer, 1880-1968

Health & Beauty Tip

DO NOT BE AN EMOTIONAL DRESSER! Even if your circumstances look dim at this time, hold on, seasons always change and this too shall pass. DRESS YOUR BEST TODAY! Dress how you want to feel; get all decked out. Ladies, wear your high heels today, put on your best dress, do up your makeup just a bit. (Don't go overboard, less is more at times.) Spend a few extra minutes on yourself and walk with your head high and full of confidence knowing you will conquer your enemy.

"Regardless of how you feel inside, always try to look like a winner. Even if you are behind, a sustained look of control and confidence can give you a mental edge that results in victory."

— Arthur Ashe

Day 5

*Now to Him who is able to do immeasurably more
than all we ask or imagine, according to His power
that is at work within us...*

Ephesians 3:20
(New International Version)

Forgiveness is not an option; it is essential to living life above the ordinary. When we hold unforgiveness in our heart, we only harm ourselves and hold our offender hostage. How is this true you ask? I was molested, from the ages of 3-13, by two people close to me. This was devastating for me, however, I never realized the depth of the damaging emotional impact that these events had on my life until adolescence. I had to learn to forgive and forget; in this instance, there are so many variables, as I am sure many abused women face and even question.

I am here to talk about the freedom, not the bondage. After many years, as I matured in ministry, I opened myself up for healing. I talked to my pastors, who helped nurture my walk with God. I was able to share this testimony at a women's meeting at length. I was astonished at the amount of women holding onto the grudges, the guilt, the shame, the rejection...you name a deadly emotion and it showed up. In fact, I think I faced so many of them, that it compelled my heart to always forgive and desire the freedom of others.

Forgiveness was a choice; once I made that choice, I gave God something to work with and He set me free. My freedom allowed this person, who had abused me, to come forward at the end of a meeting to receive their freedom. They accepted Christ into their heart and repented of their sin. As of today,

I am only by God's grace, afforded the privilege of maintaining a healthy relationship with this individual. For me, I found that my freedom is the fundamental of life, for without it, one can never be satisfied.

"To forgive is to set a prisoner free and discover that the prisoner was you."

— Lewis B. Smedes

Health & Beauty Tip

Make sure you use perfume on all the places that hold in fragrance. You will want to put it behind your ears, on your neck and wrist, and behind your knees. Another trick is to put perfume on a cotton ball and place it in your bra. Like the woman who poured her oil on Jesus' feet, pour your praise on God and allow His presence to manifest freedom in your life. Be patient with yourself.

"The fragrance always stays in the hand that gives the rose."

— Hada Bejar

Day 6

A cheerful disposition is good for your health; gloom and doom leave you bone-tired.

Prov. 17:22
(The Message)

Today I want you to start with the simple things. Do not dread today. God gave you today and it will be a great day; it is what you make of it. For instance, what makes you laugh, may be a temporary key to giving you the boost of endurance you need for a specific task today.

Webster says that "ENDURANCE" is the ability to last, to stand pain. This tells me that pain is subject to me. I can stand against pain and make my flesh submit to my will with help of a positive spirit within me. My spirit is laughing, but if I do not send that message to my natural flesh, my brain, I cannot laugh out loud and hear joy coming from me. When I hear this joy, I am compelled to jumpstart my physical body because of a natural reaction, resulting in positive action causing me to achieve phenomenal results in everything I put my efforts to.

You too, can have this happen to you. Just start to think of a happy memory, like the first day you accepted Christ into your heart, the first day you felt great peace, great joy, great love and forgiveness. You can do it, because with God all things are possible! Have a great day, don't loose your cool and have your joy stolen from you. Life is too short...live free today!

"A laugh is a smile that bursts."

– Mary H. Waldrip

Health & Beauty Tip

A great smile goes a long way; smile lots today…but if your pearly whites are not so white, then try this tip: Brush your teeth at least twice a day to get them their cleanest, using effective flossing. (I like the threader floss, it works great). At night, after your teeth are clean, (approx. 2 minutes of good brushing time is sufficient) use a bleaching tray (see your dentist) or use the over the counter whitening strips. My dentist said it is not a myth; they do work, however, if you feel you're getting irritation, consult with your dentist instead.

"You grow up the day you have your first real laugh at yourself."

– Ethel Barrymore

 **Day 7**

I praise you because I am fearfully
and wonderfully made; your works are wonderful,
I know that full well."

Ps. 139:4
(New International Version)

What does age have to do with intimacy...everything! Webster's definition of intimate says is quite well: a belonging to or characterizing one's deepest nature or marked by a warm friendship developing through long association. As we mature, so do our bodies and our mindsets. As years go by, we (I am speaking for most of us ladies here...) learn that life is what we make of it. How we embrace its challenges with grace and optimism is empowering, knowing that with God all things are possible.

As we grow into a more intimate relationship with Him, we are strengthened to look beyond ourselves and look into the life of another, building lasting relationships, because we know the foundation of where they originated...the Cross. I can only say from experience that the most lasting, strong, fulfilled relationships I have are with those who understand their place in life.

My mother has taught me a lot about living, not just about life. I have gained insight into her world and I am challenged to grow. The older she became, the more life brought her and the more grace she developed. I believe, as women, we have much to offer; it is our perception that really makes the difference. As we age, we can look at how our behinds are no longer sitting in the place they used to be (unless you have a serious personal trainer and a very strict diet...or lipo) haha...but really, let's face it ladies, our bodies change and so does everything else.

As I reflect back, I can almost become embarrassed at the ways I used to act, but in all reality, this is great; I have matured. I have recognized that I only get better with age. I am so much fuller of life now than when I was a little girl. I really encourage you ladies, matured women, to train a younger generation...there is a gap so wide and so empty needing to be filled. Will you help fill it?

I love to learn, listen and embrace new relationships as God brings them into my life. I encourage you to do the same. Try not to duplicate exactly what you are; not everything we know is worthy of duplication, yet everything we understand, through God's love and His Word, will always change another lady's life. There are so many little girls out there needing mothers, needing love and intimacy...at times it may cause them to find it in the wrong places.

Please hear my heart today and the heart of Father God; extend love today. Don't reflect on all the things you want to change about yourself as you mature. Focusing on the needs of others, allows clear introspection of our world to be possible. Be blessed! May favor be with you today and always!

"Age is something that doesn't matter, unless you are a cheese."

– Billie Burke

Health & Beauty Tip

Nix the face lift, unless you already have one, try grooming your eyebrows instead… they give a natural lift to the face… perhaps take a younger lady with you to the day spa or salon the next time you go and teach her how to be a lady…loving her through to maturity with God's help.

"An archaeologist is the best husband a woman can have. The older she gets the more interested he is in her."

– Agatha Christie

Day 8

But if you harbor bitter envy and selfish ambition in your hearts, do not boast about it or deny the truth. 15Such "wisdom" does not come down from heaven but is earthly, unspiritual, of the devil. 16For where you have envy and selfish ambition, there you find disorder and every evil practice. 17But the wisdom that comes from heaven is first of all pure; then peace-loving, considerate, submissive, full of mercy and good fruit, impartial and sincere.

James 3:14-17
(New International Version)

Remove all emotional toxins. Take a few moments today and evaluate yourself. What is keeping you from being kind to your boss, your co-worker, your children or spouse, etc.? Meditate on this scripture in James. I know that people have a tendency to be quick to lash out. Sharp and hurtful words may come out at times; however, this is no excuse to retaliate.

You have to talk to your flesh and tell it to shut up! You can do this by bringing your thoughts into one place in your mind, asking God to help you with all these thoughts. Bring your thoughts captive; any thought that would exalt itself against the knowledge of God...those thought do not belong to you. Give them over to God, How? Just ask God, believe God and trust Him to help your flesh be subject to the Sprit of God within you. This process will help you see the people around you in a more intimate way; you will have your mind cleared of negative thoughts, replacing them with positive thoughts.

21

Before you know it, your heart with be filled with warm-fuzzies to give out to all those people who came against you. Love never fails. In I Corinthians chapter 13, you find the way of real love. When you learn that it is easy to teach your flesh to obey your sprit and give love consistently, you will feel great every day of your life.

"Being a lady is an attitude."

— Chuck Woolery

Health & Beauty Tip

Get out of yourself and send a card or flowers to someone who may have done you wrong! Love never fails. I bet you are thinking, "How is this a beauty or health tip?" Well, it is healthy to your soul and it will beautify your spirit. Not every thing is a natural concept, some things come from the spirit and this rejuvenates us even more.

"When you can't find anything to wear...
put on love."

— Carla Riche

Day 9

Study to show thyself approved
unto God a workman that
needeth not to be ashamed,
rightly dividing the word of truth.

2 Timothy 2:15
(King James Version)

How much do you learn? Do you take time out and feed your brain? Most of us have excuses such as, "I worked all day," "I am too busy," "The kids need me." The demands are endless. Well, so is your brain power. You will only get out of it what you put into it. Knowledge is power...how much do you have? Learning is like wearing a pair of 3-D glasses–it gives dimension to your existence.

The more you know, the more colorful your world becomes, the broader your horizons are. I used to be afraid to study or learn; in fact, I can remember numerous times in college when I would call in sick because I had a verbal quiz or presentation to make. I was afraid to see the 3-D world, afraid that I would flop. The only reason I would flop was because I did not use my brain power and study the way I knew I had to, resulting in lack of discipline, causing great disappointment.

In essence, all of this fear was a root of rejection that I felt as a child and I had to receive great inner healing from Jesus to receive the true fact that I really was smart and I could not be rejected when I do it in God's strength. No longer do I suffer from that fear. I am FREE. "Whom the Son has set free is free indeed." I know I have the power within me; NOT MY

POWER, but the Bible says I do not have a spirit of fear but of power, love and of a SOUND MIND.

In other words, I have His power working in me and I can achieve great results all the time! I have discipline - I love to learn when I read; it makes me feel productive. I can enter so many conversations and have something worthwhile to say. Take this scripture and quote it. Read it and memorize it for the next seven days. On Day 16, check in to see how much you remember.

"I always keep myself in a position of being a student."

— Jackie Joyner-Kersee,
track athlete

Health & Beauty Tip

Expose yourself and get some knowledge for your body. Sometimes the only skin that gets attention is the skin that shows: the face and hands. Skin can be neglected if we get too busy; put lotion on your entire body twice daily. It takes less than five minutes and you can do this in the AM after your shower and at night before you go to bed. Exfoliate with a body scrub in the shower, also, while you have conditioner in your hair. Remember, taking care of every part of your body is just as important as your soul.

"Nothing you learn, however wide of the mark it may appear at the time or however trivial, is ever wasted."

— Eleanor Roosevelt,
First Lady, humanitarian,
1884-1962

Day 10

We call Abraham "father" not because he got God's attention by living like a saint, but because God made something out of Abraham when he was a nobody. Isn't that what we've always read in Scripture, God saying to Abraham, "I set you up as father of many peoples"? Abraham was first named "father" and then became a father because he dared to trust God to do what only God could do: raise the dead to life, with a word make something out of nothing.

Romans 4:17
(The Message)

Your words have the right to declare or to create anything you want. Ok, I am not talking about some "name it and claim it" phrase...I am talking about those things that benefit and profit the spirit, if you speak them out boldly. Now you cannot have authority and boldness in purity, speaking things out, if you do not even know who you are in Christ. That is a whole different subject. But do not be discouraged; start today and start with proclaiming boldly that you are fearfully and wonderfully made.

If you want the blessings you must obey! OUCH! I know that one hurt, but you have to walk in obedience in order to receive God's blessings over your life. You cannot live like the devil and expect to speak things into the atmosphere and get great results. You can not be hypocritical against the Word of God; you must be obedient and then you will experience great breakthroughs.

"Words kill, words give life; they're either poison or fruit - you choose."

Proverbs 18:21
(The Message)

Health & Beauty Tip

Try extending your comfort zone and being a bit bolder with your eye shadow. I am not talking about looking like Madonna; I am just suggesting you try a bolder color on your eyelids. I favor the MAC cosmetics counter and I have, at times, asked the girls there to take a few minutes and show me the latest colors and what would look the best on my face. So be bold enough to wear a new color and bold enough to ask someone for help. Try it, I bet you'll love the change.

"Kind words are a creative force, a power that concurs in the building up of all that is good, and energy that showers blessings upon the world."

– Lawrence G. Lovasik

Day 11

Wherever your treasure is, there your heart
and thoughts will also be.

Mt. 6:21
(New Living Translation)

Take notice of where your heart is today…one good parallel I can use is my husband. He is my treasure; I want to do the best I can to protect that, to preserve that and walk in total love, with genuine intimacy in my heart for him. It is easy to do when I am aware daily of how much of a treasure he really is.

Take notice again of your treasure; are you treating it/them like trash? If so, re-group and breathe in a moment and get refreshed. How? Take a moment, turn on some worship music and be quiet, allowing the Holy Sprit to minister to you. If you allow Him to, He will bring to your remembrance those things that you need to work on. Do not be discouraged, but rather encouraged, knowing all things work together for good to them that love the Lord.

"If you have only one smile in you,
give it to the people you love. Don't be surly at
home, then go out in the street and start grinning
"Good morning" at total strangers."

– Maya Angelou

Health & Beauty Tip

Date night with my "hottie" (married folks only), scheduling time one night a week, is valuable in discovering each other's wonderful uniqueness. David and I take at least one night a week for just US; no phones, no faxes, no emails, just us. Sometimes we just stay home and cuddle.

"Kind words can be short and easy to speak, but their echoes are truly endless."

– Mother Teresa

Day 12

For God did not give us a spirit of timidity
(of cowardice, of craven and cringing and
fawning fear), but [He has given us a spirit] of
power and of love and of calm and well-balanced
mind and discipline and self-control.

2 Tim. 1:7
(The Amplified Bible)

It is said in God's Word that we do not have to fear anything…when we recognize that, we have the mind of Christ and get a true meaning of this deep in our spirits; we can live fear free. How do we get the true meaning of this? By spending quality time with God. How is your prayer time? Only you can determine how intimate your relationship with God really is; the deeper you go, the more you grow.

"You gain strength, courage and confidence
by every experience in which you really
stop to look fear in the face.
You must do the thing which you
think you cannot do."

– Eleanor Roosevelt

Health & Beauty Tip

Discipline yourself to set out your outfits for the next day, the night before. Ever have those last minute mornings? Oh no! What shoes do I wear? My hair won't go with that outfit? Make it easy and breezy in the AM. Help yourself out the night before.

"I moved to New York City for my health. I'm paranoid and New York was the only place where my fears were justified."

– Eleanor Roosevelt

Day 13

Do not seek revenge or bear a grudge against one of your people, but love your neighbor as yourself. I am the LORD.

Lev. 19:18
(New International Version)

This scripture may be hard for a few, but I believe you can catch the revelation and really be honest with yourself today. If you are wondering why it is hard to love your friend, spouse, etc., it is because you don't love yourself. How can you love someone else when you have hatred toward your own body?

You are created in the image and likeness of God; everything He created is good. You have the right lips, hips and fingertips God wanted you to have. Now, I am aware that some of you may have enlarged some areas on your own....hold off and don't get mad at yourself. Stop eating 12 Twinkies a night and find out the real root of your food problem. Food does not take the place of healing; only inner healing comes from God.

What is it you keep disliking about yourself (I am only talking to those individuals reading this who are not free...all of you who are free and love your self as Christ loves you, celebrate with another and pray for your neighbor.) I encourage you to find out what it is that you dislike and then find scriptures in the Bible that counteract those thoughts and quote them over yourself daily OR seek wise counsel to assist you into the process of loving yourself again.

See, I know I am talking to a little girl who once loved, but got hurt and then felt unlovable and in turn you have carried that baggage with you, causing you to dislike yourself. God forgives you, but you must forgive yourself, along with forgiving those who have hurt you. God has the best for you and wants you to be totally free.

"Our lives improve only when we take chances –
and the first and most difficult risk we can take
is to be honest with ourselves."

– Walter Anderson
(b. 1944), American writer

Health & Beauty Tip

Treat yourself to a home pedicure, unless you have the extra money without going into debt...then go to the salon and have fun. This will not take the place of your inner healing, but your feet will sure look good in the process. HAHA~

"I don't have false teeth. Do you think I'd buy teeth like these?"

– Carol Burnett

Day 14

And whenever you stand praying
if you have anything against anyone, forgive him
and let it drop (leave it, let it go),
in order that your Father Who is in heaven
may also forgive you your
[own] failings and shortcomings and let them drop.

Mk. 11:25
(The Amplified Bible)

A subject many want to ignore, but extremely necessary for complete freedom! Without forgiveness, you rob yourself of successful thoughts, resulting in positive actions. You rob yourself of the truth. I know because, for years in the past, I would reflect on who did me wrong, what church had burned me, what staff member left me, how I was mistreated and misunderstood.

Do you see the negative pattern it creates? This sounds depressing, doesn't it? Are you in the same place today? Only you can be honest with yourself. Besides, you can't lie to God anyway; He created you and He really knows the truth. I can reassure you, though, that forgiveness is definitely the key, the way out. If God forgave you of all your dirty laundry, then how could you possibly hold unforgiveness in your heart toward someone else?

Well, the answer is really easy. Hurting people hurt other people. But FREE people want to set others free too! If I were to expound here on all the amazing things I have learned through the art of forgiveness, this would not be a devotional, but a novel. However, if you want to know more, I do have a tape series called, "The Resurrected Woman," in which I go into detail about my total freedom.

I hold no grudges. I have great respect for people who are real; who can identify with the real problem and seek the real answer…Jesus Christ! So just be encouraged today. Learn to forgive and take baby steps if you have to…God will never give you more than you can handle. I believe in you and know you can forgive.

"Life appears to me to be too short to be spent in nursing animosity or registering wrong."

– Charlotte Brontë

Health & Beauty Tip

Beautify from within…write a letter. Not just any letter; write one to someone you are still holding unforgiveness against. Now, I do suggest that you do not give this letter to the individual, rather use it as a tool to help you overcome this grievance. After you are finished writing, take a moment, take a deep breath and then read the issues of your heart. You will then know what to do. You will see if this is a silly thing keeping you from forgiving or if it is so serious that you are utterly shocked at what you wrote. If the latter is the case, then take it to the Lord in prayer and ask Him to take this from you. Close your eyes and just begin to worship God and allow His healing power to manifest in your heart. Remember that weeping may endure for the night, but joy comes in the morning.

"Say what you want about long dresses, but they cover a multitude of shins."

— Mae West

Journal

Day 15

Understand [this], my beloved brethren
Let every man be quick to hear [a ready listener],
slow to speak, slow to take offense and to get angry.

Jam. 1:19
(The Amplified Bible)

I am sure that no one has ever had a bad day, whatsoever! I can recall a few, just a few...haha. It is very important to know that a kind word turns away wrath. It is easy to be aware of this if you recognize that you must listen when someone speaks and not speak over them. That way you can effectively be able to interpret the real meaning of what is being spoken. If you do not, the cat claws will comes out (rrreeerrhh!).

So, my friends, listen up and have enough strength, no matter how much you may want to jump into a conversation to quickly state your point, hold your peace and let the other person speak. When we really listen to someone, they begin to expose the issues of their own heart. If you will only listen close enough, you will save yourself from a great bit of strife and contention.

Your task for the day is to muzzle your mouth! Not that you can't speak, just have the strength to listen. Besides being a good listener, the people that listen long enough normally get paid for it (psychologists)!

"The first duty of love is to listen."

– Paul Tillich

Health & Beauty Tip

Take some time-out to listen to some music that will soothe your soul. I personally like Frank Sinatra. In fact, David and I sometimes play the music and ballroom dance around our living room. Have fun with it and enjoy yourself!

"Listening is an attitude of the heart, a genuine desire to be with another which both attracts and heals."

– J. Isham

Journal

Day 16

Instead, be kind to each other,
tenderhearted, forgiving one another,
just as God through Christ has forgiven you.

Eph. 4:32
(New Living Translation)

Now this can be hard to do! Love, be tender-hearted, forgiving as Christ did for me…oh shoot, I have to do it! It is God's Word, but it is not easy. I love my husband with all of my heart, but how can I be tender when he is being a grump? Come on, I'll bet you are beginning to think of someone you know who's grumpy, aren't you? Ok, maybe not, but if you are, let me help you.

You see that was what the "old" Christine was like. If "I" be "in" Christ, I am a "new" creature. Behold, all things have passed away and all things have become new. I am no longer concerned with what David does, he belongs to God, not me; I am just his helpmate and an asset to him, not a burden. So, it is possible to be kind, I did it. I would go out and get David a card if he was fussy with me for something and write the kindest, most loving things from my heart. (Now, I had to make my mind think of these nice things in the middle of wanting to be fussy myself.) It is easy now, hard back then…now I just bring every thought into captivity, anything that would exalt itself against the knowledge of God and say, "MIND, ACT RIGHT!"

God would want you to act right, be right and stay right; it's hard at first, but with practice it becomes easy. Try it, you can do it! When I would give David those cards, he would melt about four hours later, but every good snowman has to go down sooner or later. The light and love of my heart was too much for him not to accept. I loved him when he seemed unlovable and he, in turn, would do the same for me.

Today, I experience love on a consistent basis, freely. So, do I have a bad day? Sure, do I get angry? Yup, from time to time, but I sin NOT in the process and I am never angry for more than 20 minutes tops! You can achieve it too. I am not some super woman; just a woman after God's own heart! Practice it today and see what happens for you!

"Concern is only worry within a tuxedo; you can dress it up, but it is still the same thing."

– Anonymous

Health & Beauty Tip

Smile! Smile lots and smile big today. It takes more muscles to frown than it does to smile and it ages you quicker. So chin up and stay youthful. While practicing a big smile in the mirror today before you leave the house, get a mental picture of your smile and let it stay in the forefront of your mind.

40

"My mother buried three husbands – and two of them were only napping."

– Rita Rudner

Day 17

Declare me innocent, O LORD,
for I have acted with integrity;
I have trusted in the LORD without wavering.

Ps. 26:1
(New Living Translation)

If you hate your job and don't want to go today, get up and go anyway! If you are really unhappy, figure out why? Is this job just convenient or close to the house? I don't know, but you do. If you like your job, then help your co-workers around you like theirs too. There was a time in my life when I had to make a job change, for a whole lot less money than expected! However, for me, I knew this was God because He wanted to teach me so many things, mainly how to endure to the end.

I am not telling you to leave your job or find a place that pays less; I am just letting you know what I had to do at one point in my life. Had I decided to give up and not endure until the end, I would have missed out on the biggest blessing ever and that was the opportunity to meet my husband, David!

Even though I got treated like a dog "for a brief" moment (and some of it was a result of my "attitude") still there was no justification for the lack of respect and lack of pay I received. But so many lessons came out of my endurance. I not only met David, but when God blessed me with the staff team I have now... I made a commitment to not muzzle the ox, a workmen is worthy of his hire, regardless of what they are portraying at that moment. I believe God brought me my team, whether they had faults or not and I recognized it was part of my assignment to help them be set free too!

*"Endure the present,
and watch for better things."*

– Virgil

Health & Beauty Tip

Exercising builds muscle, so endure, even if it hurts. If you want your reward, you have to endure. My trainer told me to be consistent with my workouts, if not, after 21 days of not exercising, my muscle dumps its memory. I do not want that, so I suck it up and endure; as a result, I have pretty good looking arms now!

"He who laughs last didn't get it."

– Helen Giangregorio

Day 18

Put on God's whole armor [the armor of a heavy-armed soldier which God supplies], that you may be able successfully to stand up against [all] the strategies and the deceits of the devil.

Eph. 6:11
(The Amplified Bible)

Great strength can be drawn in the midst of adversity. But without your armor, it is hard to withstand the works of the devil! Ok, I am not getting fruity on you; just bringing you back to the basics. No good soldier goes to battle without arming themselves first. They come ready dressed for battle. Every day the devil is seeking for those whom he may devour. May he devour you? Do you have your armor on or not?

I'm not saying that you have to be a devil chaser, but have an awareness of the spirit realm, knowing that God has already gone before you, but you must do your part and wear your armor. I verbally put it on as an act of faith daily! I notice a big difference walking around protected than if I were caught in the woods with my pants down…A merry heart works good like a medicine and helps the battle seem easier to win.

"Sometimes your medicine bottle has on it, 'Shake well before using.' That is what God has to do with some of His people. He has to shake them well before they are ever usable."

– Vance Havner

Health & Beauty Tip

Dress appropriately for all occasions. If it is winter, please do yourself a favor and cover up. My mother always taught me that if my head and my feet were covered, I would always be warm.

"Stop thinking about your difficulties, whatever they are, and start thinking about God instead."

— Emmet Fox

Day 19

The apostles returned to Jesus from their ministry tour and told him all they had done and what they had taught. 31Then Jesus said, "Let's get away from the crowds for a while and rest." There were so many people coming and going that Jesus and his apostles didn't even have time to eat.

Mark 6:30, 31
(New Living Translation)

Take time out of your busyness for you. Learn that you can only push yourself so far before you snap...crackle & pop! Learn the art of relaxation and regrouping. If you're feeling overwhelmed, stop for a moment and vacate your circumstances, get a group of advisors, counselor or leaders whom you trust and bounce off of them what's on your mind. Most of the time, all we really need is time in God's presence–for refreshing, someone to just listen to help you sort out these issues; clarity comes when counsel is given.

"Who among us hasn't envied a cat's ability to ignore the cares of daily life and to relax completely?"

– Karen Brademeyer

Health & Beauty Tip

Get some expert advice via book, church counsel, teaching tapes on subjects that you know would benefit your life. Applied knowledge is power... remember, always take the meat and throw out the bones. Find what works best for you and work your stuff.

"A vacation frequently means that the family goes away for a rest, accompanied by a mother who sees that the others get it."

— Marcelene Cox

Day 20

There is a time for everything,
and a season for every activity under heaven.

Ecclesiastes 3:1

I once read a quote that really stood out to me, it read like this: "You don't know a woman until you have had a letter from her." How many times have you thought about your childhood girlfriends, a loved one, reminisced about an old relationship that really touched your heart? Numerous, I am sure and how many times have we neglected to express to that person our feelings of gratefulness? Take a moment today and write a letter to this someone; extending a bit of held-in warm-fuzzies to someone who has impacted your life in a meaningful way is a great place to start.

I encourage you not to dwell on stinky relationships...ones that you know are not for you! I am talking about someone who really made a deposit of wealth into your life. For example, some years back I took time and wrote a letter to one of my college teachers, Mrs. Gail Lambert; she really impacted my life when I first attended school. I went back to college in my twenties and I felt a little out of sorts...Mrs. Lambert was so gentle and affirming. Her grace helped me see the real purpose of being there. I was invited to her house for some coffee and my eyes were opened to a different view of the so-called "COLLEGE WORLD." Because I chose to go back to school in my later years, I was very determined to get the most out it. The sorority girls and parties had not peaked my interest in that season, therefore, Mrs. Lambert did.

In writing to her, I had expressed the ways in which she impacted my life and thanked her for her efforts to see the best in others. To my surprise, I received a letter back, stating how proud she was of me and how far I had come. This letter came at the right time, the right day and I was glad that I took the time out of my busy life to let her know I care. Now from time to time, I go back and read her letter; call me sentimental, but it really is great to read the love from her heart and it helps me keep going forward.

"What a lot we lost when we stopped writing letters. You can't reread a phone call."

— Liz Carpenter

Health & Beauty Tip

Beautify yourself from the inside out; let your heart show! Send a card to someone you love. Thank someone today for impacting your life in a positive way. I encourage you, if you are married - DO NOT WAIT until FEB. 14th to express your love, do it today; surprise your spouse with a wonderful surprise from your heart. The rest of you, just send flowers, if your budget allows or just simply write a letter and mail it this week.

"I am a little pencil in the hand of a writing God who is sending a love letter to the world."

— Mother Teresa

Good Morning Your Highness

Day 21

God is faithful and reliable.
If we confess our sins, He forgives them and
cleanses us from everything we've done wrong.

I John 1:9
(Gods Word Translation)

If you are like most girls, you may sometimes feel cranky, angry, depressed or sad. Now, as women of God, we are taught we should not confess such things. In other words, we should not speak negativity such as, "I am having a bad day" or "I feel depressed" etc., however, reality is, you face these feelings from time to time and then act on those feelings throughout your day, don't you? The next time you get bent out of shape emotionally, be patient and give it to God. Being honest with yourself takes courage.

You must realize that if you have done something or someone wrong or if you acted like a jerk today and you blew it, then take a moment and realize God's mercy and grace are there to forgive you, but you must first recognize what you did and make a conscious effort TO NOT reflect the same actions (words, gestures, thoughts, to name a few). God will forgive you, but you must come to grips with reality and face the truth of your error.

"If we had no winter,
the spring would not be so pleasant."

– Anne Bradstreet,
poet 1612-1672

Health & Beauty Tip

Get a FACIAL: Peeling off old layers of dead skin cells rejuvenates our face and gives us a healthy glow. The same is true with our time in the presence of God. When we take time, quality time, not 25 minutes of driving time to our destination, but real time with God, His presence can be reflected on us. Our face will have a glow, because we have ditched old "feeling cranky" emotions and we feel rejuvenated spiritually. (Home facials work also...do not go into debt and spend $60 to get a facial if you do not have the funds to do so at this time. Be patient, be a tither, a giver, be obedient...increase is coming!)

"The basic trouble with depression is that it is so depressing. It often helps to look on the bright side. Make a teensy list of things that have not happened, that really would be depressing if they had."

— Miss Piggy, Muppet

Day 22

Jesus prayed, "Father, forgive them;
they don't know what they're doing."
Dividing up his clothes, they threw dice for them.

Lu. 23:34
(The Message)

There are many ways in which an individual can express forgiveness. I have used many methods such as a soft, kind phone call, addressing the issue in a loving matter. I have sent anything from flowers, to cards, to faxes. You name it. In fact, I am so 100% sure that forgiving people is such a freedom that many don't have, I am always going out of my way to take the high road. I am not one of these, "I'm sorry people," if I have done nothing wrong; I just choose that if someone's done me wrong, I immediately go to them and tell them I forgive them...it actually shocks most people. Especially if they are really guilty, it hits 'em between the eyes.

I encourage you today, if someone happens to do you wrong, immediately go to them and take that moment to resolve the issue. Life is too short to hold onto unforgiveness...no matter who started the problem; someone will always have to take the high road. Why not let it be you?

"Forgiveness is the act of admitting
we are like other people."

– Christina Baldwin

Health & Beauty Tip

Sleek Physique: Stay away from salty food as much as possible. Salt causes your body to retain water, making the skin look puffy and bloated.

"You will know that forgiveness has begun when you recall those who hurt you and feel the power to wish them well."

– Lewis B. Smedes

Day 23

A final word: Be strong with the Lord's mighty power.

Ephesians 6:10
(New Living Translation)

There is strength in numbers and I am referring to the strength gained by loved ones around you. I have noticed, many times in my life, that who I surround myself with is a reflection of what I become. People are like elevators; they can take you up or take you down. Who do you have surrounding you?

I challenge you today to have the strength to observe the people around you. Who do you talk to, shop with, let in your home...who is your best friend? You know these answers, stop and think about it for a moment. How do you feel around these people? Do you feel uplifted, energetic, revived and accepted for your "true" self? If not, I would be re-evaluating who I camp with! I once had a few wrong people in my life. I asked God to help remove them; I stood in faith, believing that if I walked in love, God would answer my prayer. HE DID! I'm continually discerning the right people in my life.

"Become wise by walking with the wise; hang out with fools and watch your life fall to pieces."

Proverbs 13:20
(The Message Bible)

Health & Beauty Tip

Celebrate your differences from another; learn to see other people from the inside out. I recognize gifts in others and celebrate that, but I am also wise enough to know that, even though I see their gift, not every one has to be unwrapped by me. I love all people because it is a mantle on my life and more importantly God commands me to, however, I do not have to take everyone to the mall with me. Watch who you hang out with, but never loose sight of celebration!

"Associate with men (or women) of good quality, if you esteem your own reputation; for it is better to be alone than in bad company."

– George Washington

Day 24

Don't use foul or abusive language.
Let everything you say be good and helpful, so that your
words will be an encouragement to those who hear them.

Eph. 4:29
(New Living Translation)

Tame your tongue! We can never talk about this subject too much. Everyday, we all have an opportunity to watch what we say and how we say it. I pray daily that the words of my mouth and the meditation of my heart would be pleasing and acceptable in God's sight. I ask you today to say this same prayer over yourself (Psalms 19:14). It takes discipline to be silent; silence can never be misquoted, never!

It is better to be silent and look wise, than open up your mouth and look foolish. No matter what you face today, a board meeting, a PTA meeting, a staff meeting or just plain conversations, watch what you say. Make a conscious effort to listen before you speak; evaluate your answer in your brain, with the consulting of the Holy Spirit, then speak. Keeping in mind to be quick to listen and slow to speak. That is the key that will lead you to the peak of your day.

"Because a woman's vocal cords are shorter than a man's she can actually speak with less effort than he can. Shorter vocal cords not only cause a woman's voice to be more highly pitched, but also require less air to become agitated, making it possible for her to talk more with less energy expended."

Homemade,
December 1984.

Health & Beauty Tip

Cough it up! Stop smoking, if this applies to you. If you can not stop, then 1) Ask God for help 2) Quit for your own health 3) Quit for your skin 4) Quit for your children or loved ones who don't want to see a premature end to your life. Smoking is the second major cause of premature wrinkles. (Sun damage is first,) Nicotine constricts the small blood vessels and decreases the flow of oxygen and nutrients to your skin, so stop harming your body today!

"I personally think we developed language because of our deep inner need to complain."
– Jane Wagner

Journal

Day 25

Whatever may be your task, work at it heartily (from the soul), as [something done] for the Lord and not for men.

Col 3:23
(The Amplified Bible)

My mother is a very warm, kind-hearted woman. She is at her best when she is sharing a part of her heart with the ones she loves. I enjoy having company over. I love the art of hospitality. All of this I have learned from my mother. I reflect on all the values and hidden truths that I have learned from my mother's life. I have watched this women go through some very hard times; times that could have sent her bags packing, right to the mental ward.

I look at the most beautiful reflection of God's love, grace and forgiveness when I look into her eyes. She shares an intimate place in her heart with all those that she comes in contact with. I love her for that. I encourage you to be vulnerable enough, in spite what life has dealt you, to step out of yourself and into the intimacy of letting someone else into your heart. It changes people and helps them see that they are real and that you are real...life is not about being fake. Fake things, if given enough time, always break.

"Giving frees us from the familiar territory of our own needs by opening our mind to the unexplained worlds occupied by the needs of others."

– Barbara Bush

Health & Beauty Tip

Take it slow…showers can be just as relaxing as a bath, if not done in a hurry. Let the steamy, warm shower be soothing and relaxing. Linger a bit longer, don't rush and let the water (I like mine a bit on the hot side) massage your tense muscles. Two extra minutes in the morning will set the ease factor for the day.

"The love we give away is the only love we keep."

– Elbert Hubbard

Day 26

Take good counsel and accept correction– that's the way to live wisely and well. Listening to advice has long-term benefits. Wisdom compounds itself over time.

Prov. 19:20
(The Message)

It is very important to learn that no one person is an island by themselves. It takes strength to seek the advice of wise counselors. I seek those who have the values I desire to have imparted into my life; people with integrity and purity who will not compromise truth. I would rather have truth in helping me make a solid decision, no matter how much it may pierce me; truth with love is the only way out. I am not my own identity, an island on my own. I have a home church, a pastor, a board of advisors for the ministry and a board of advisors for our business. I seek wise counsel and benefit greatly from the team effort I have before me.

How many of you are your own island? Are you without a home church, an advisor, a pastor, someone in authority over you? Many have rebelled against this because of pride and self-awareness. We do not have all the answers all the time. This is why the Bible says that there is wisdom and safety in the multitude of counsel. In the business arena, advisors are selected to help aid in the company's decision making, giving profitable results. The actual decision is left up to the CEO of the corporation; however, without the help of the selected advisors, the CEO would not have been able to make a solid, sound decision. This tells me that the same structure for our everyday life is necessary.

For example, have you ever gone to a counselor, a therapist, a psychologist seeking advice on a certain situation? Most of us have and if you haven't yet, this may be the reason why you have not come out of this situation with freedom. Wise decision making is rarely a solo performance. Effective leaders surround themselves with people who can provide accurate information, most likely in a timely manner with insight to the meaning of the information, as well as offering suggestions and advice about the most effective action to take.

In the end result, the leader has to make the last call, however the advice, wisdom and sound counsel comes from a team effort. I encourage you to hold yourself accountable and realize there is safety in numbers. No football team fights against itself; there must be an offense and defense to make an effective game profitable. So, if you do not have a home church or someone over you to advise you, please find them today.

"Anyone who stops learning is old,
whether at twenty or eighty.
Anyone who keeps learning stays young.
The greatest thing in life
is to keep your mind young."
– Henry Ford

Health & Beauty Tip

When shopping, don't just buy the first thing you see, get the advice of other sales associates in the store to direct you in the event of an upcoming sale, a discount for that day or to another brand that may be less expensive but "equal in quality."

"When seeking wise counsel, I would not go to my dentist to fix my car. Find the right counsel for your exact situation, keeping in mind, the best counsel are those who seek the counsel of the Lord for themselves.

— Christine Martin

Day 27

And let us not lose heart and grow weary and faint
in acting nobly and doing right, for in due time
and at the appointed season we shall reap,
if we do not loosen and relax our courage and faint.

Gal. 6:9
(The Amplified Bible)

Growing up, I was raised to think on my own... to my parents' dismay; I took that to the extreme, thinking my parents did not know anything. Mom's, this one is for you, HOLD ON, I SAY!!! I am a wonderful example of God's grace, mercy and love today. I have grown into a beautiful woman of God. I must say, my mother has had to hold (or should I say grip) onto this Scripture with everything that was in her, knowing that God would be faithful to complete that which He started in me. My mother learned that I belonged to God and He was obligated to take care of me. My mother teaches women all around the world on how to love your children and let them go! "Give them roots & give them wings!"

Let your child go into the hands of God. My mother would tell you, if you asked her, this was one of the hardest things to do as a mother, but it is possible. When she did, the rest was history. Today my mother works by my side and is a major asset to our ministry. She often travels with me and has the profound opportunity to teach other Moms this wonderful art of letting go and letting God have His way! As my friend Lisa Bevere puts it, "Out of control and loving it."

"The way I see it, if you want the rainbow,
you gotta put up with the rain."

— Dolly Parton

Health & Beauty Tip

If you want to change the way you look and you're on your way to eating healthy, then hold on. I am sure you didn't gain the weight overnight; therefore it will not be "poof-it's-gone" overnight. You will reap if you faint not. So don't be weary, stay consistent with your healthy eating habits and take the word "DIET" out of your vocabulary; this messes us all up...we have to change our lifestyle into eating right.

"The best way to keep children at home is to make the home atmosphere pleasant – and let the air out of their tires."

— Dorothy Parke

Journal

Day 28

A person without self-control is like a house
with its doors and windows knocked out.

Pr. 25:28
(The Message)

Tell your flesh NO from your own spirit. Be filled with the Spirit of God and have self control. May you be repulsed by every evil work. I understand that this may sound harsh, however, in order to grow, you must say no! Not everything that looks good is good; be wise and discern where you go and what you do. I am assuming here that you are a mature woman of God, wanting the things of God to be manifest in your life and this does not come without a price.

Anything great, full of quality has a price. You can either buy a cubic zirconia for $99.00 or hold off the real deal at a much "higher" price. I am not saying here, that you can not wear costume jewelry; I am just trying to make a natural parallel to the Spirit. I know you know the right thing to do today. Walk a life that is pleasing and acceptable to God. Walk after the fruit of the Spirit and NOT the lust of the flesh. I have, with God's help over a period of time, learned the powerful tool of utilizing Christ's power within me to resist the devil and every evil work! I practice it daily.

"Quality begins on the inside...
and then works its way out."

-- Bob Moawad

Health & Beauty Tip

Flush it out! Drinking at least eight 8 oz. glasses of water per day will flush your body of harmful toxins. Drinking it cold helps because the body has to burn more calories when the water is cold. If you are flushing out the spirit, then take some time to flush out the flesh… You may visit the bathroom a lot, but your body will thank you!

"You can't fake quality any more than you can fake a good meal."

– William S. Burroughs

Day 29

God wants us to grow up,
to know the whole truth and tell it in love–
like Christ in everything.
We take our lead from Christ,
who is the source of everything we do.

Ephesians 4:15
(The Message)

Here is a test which I know you will pass. I challenge you today; have complete integrity in every area of your life. Now, you may say you are an honest person, but what about those little white lies? You know…the ones you've told your boss… "I was stuck in traffic," when you know you left late because you had a bad hair day or the ones when you call the salon and cancel an appointment last minute because you forgot or felt too tired to get there…telling the salon some small white lie like your dog got sick and you can't make it. Integrity means wholeness, honesty and sincerity.

When was the last time you were completely honest the entire day through? I can speak from experience because I used to lie often, but I am free and it is the best feeling ever. I know you can relate, maybe not all of you reading this, but to those who are honest enough with themselves to tell the truth in this area, I commend you! This is the first step to overcoming the destructive pattern.

Let me help you. I had to pray and ask God to take this away. I had to make a conscious effort to be truthful everyday, even if it cost me something. In other words, I remember times when I would cancel an appointment and lie. Now, if I have to call, I tell the truth, cancel the appointment and then have enough integrity to offer to pay the individual for the services rendered that I requested. Most of the time, I never have to pay anyway, but I believe it was because I had enough integrity, even if it hurt at the time to say I'll pay, that God said, "Ok, I will show you grace because you are walking in obedience to My Word and it says, 'Thou shall not lie!'"

Again, I challenge and encourage you to walk with integrity today. Do it in love, not sarcastically or rudely, but just be honest and you will feel a lightness come over you throughout your entire day...this lightness is the purity of God. If God set me free from this, He can set you free too, but you have to activate your faith. Faith without works is dead...be blessed and sleep tight tonight!

"Everything you add to the truth subtracts from the truth."

– Alexander Solzhenitsyn
1918-, Russian Novelist

Health & Beauty Tip

Lying is stressful and it causes wrinkles, so if you told the truth today, treat yourself to a facial peel...peeling off dead layers of old skin cells rejuvenates the face, tightens the skin and leaves you with a very youthful and refreshed face. P.S. Do not go into debt to get the peel; often, home remedies work just as well.

"A lie gets halfway around the world before the truth has a chance to get its pants on."

– Sir Winston Churchill

Journal

Day 30

Each of you should look
not only to your own interests,
but also to the interests of others

Phil. 2:4
(New International Version)

Big boobs, no boobs, short legs, long legs, flabby tummy, no waist, short neck.....WHO CARES! You are fearfully and wonderfully made! God loves you so much He does not want us to put our confidence in our flesh, which is only a temporal thing anyway. We must learn to love ourselves in spite of our bodies. A long time ago, in my "old" me days, I was addicted to the scale. I was literally obsessed with the way I looked; I hired a trainer, I bought new clothes, I tried everything from Atkins, to soups, to the South-beach diet...no luck!

I had to take some time off and reflect on the thing that really mattered most and that was me. Not in a selfish way, but I had to realize, if I was to help others overcome indulgences and the flesh (addictions, control, manipulations, deadly emotions, just to name a few, I went through them all...), I had to truly be emptied out to be filled back up with nothing but the glory of God in my life! I had to die to my flesh and soul and learn to live completely by the Spirit within me. God has given me power and authority and has commanded me to GO and do His will, freely walking in FREEDOM!

He wants the same for you, but you must want it. How bad

do you want it? What you are willing to walk away from, determines what God will bring to you! The only way to do it is to be gut-level honest with yourself and your issues and let the loving correction of God change you forever. Whom the Son has set free is free indeed, discipleship is the process! Have a great journey; see you on the other side!

*"Only a kind person
is able to judge another justly and to make
allowances for his weaknesses.
A kind eye, while recognizing defects,
sees beyond them."*

– Lawrence G. Lovasik

Health & Beauty Tip

Meditating on God's Word for the day is a great way to boost your self-esteem and self-confidence.

"Kindness is the language which the deaf can hear and the blind can see."

– Mark Twain

Day 31

You offspring of vipers!
How can you speak good things
when you are evil (wicked)?
For out of the fullness (the overflow, the
superabundance) of the heart the mouth speaks.

Matthew 12:34
(The Amplified Bible)

When you are walking in complete freedom, you will begin to recognize the depth of how your spirit speaks (I Corinthians 10-12). I can recall a time when I was working on a very important project. I had a deadline and the time was getting close and I had just received an extra instruction of other tasks I needed to tend to for my husband, David. I wanted to put this specific task of my husband's first...I thought for a moment and before I knew it, these words came flying out of my mouth, "By this time tomorrow, I will have the entire project completed." I did not think about how, it just came to me.

The amazing thing was my words went before me to create life, to create the exact result I knew I needed and wanted. By that night, I realized I had completed both great tasks. Not even realizing that, throughout that day, I had rearranged my entire schedule to assist me in this completion. Amazing how my words caused an action and sent the message right to my brain. My spirit grabbed a hold of it and the next thing you know, I got this great revelation of how my words that were spoken boldly, created exactly what I said. Powerful isn't it?

It took me by surprise, really, when I sat down and recaptured the events of the day. I saw them re-arranged in order to line up with what I already spoke the day before. You too, can have this happen to you. I encourage you to walk after the Spirit, not the flesh. Get a real revelation of casting your cares on the Lord and He will surely take care of you! He did it for me and as a result I have received a tremendous revelation that life and death is in the power of the tongue.

*"Language exerts hidden power,
like the moon on the tides."*

– Rita Mae Brown

Health & Beauty Tip

Handle your body with care...speak life over yourself; you do deserve a break. So tonight, turn off the TV, try hard not to answer the phone and treat yourself to a bubble bath. Turn on some soft music, light a candle and just relax. Let the day reflect before you; allow tension and stress to be turned over to the hands of God...you deserve a break tonight; you will feel refreshed for the AM because you took some time for yourself!

"Why is it when we talk to God we're said to be praying, but when God talks to us we're schizophrenic?"

– Lily Tomlin

Good Morning Your Highness

Journal

For more information
about additional resources
or for booking Christine Martin for
your upcoming event please visit
www.ChristineMartin.org

P.O. Box 608150
Orlando, Florida 32860
407-629-0015

Enjoy A FREE
Copy of
*Ultimate Life
Magazine*
by visiting

www.ChristineMartin.org